# Monthly & Weekly Planner

Light and Dark Publishing

# JANUARY

| Sunday | Monday | Tuesday | Wednesday | Thursday | Friday | Saturday |
|--------|--------|---------|-----------|----------|--------|----------|
|        |        |         |           |          |        |          |
|        |        |         |           |          |        |          |
|        |        |         |           |          |        |          |
|        |        |         |           |          |        |          |
|        |        |         |           |          |        |          |
|        |        |         |           |          |        |          |

# January

- Sunday ☐
- Monday ☐
- Tuesday ☐
- Wednesday ☐
- Thursday ☐
- Friday ☐
- Saturday ☐

# January

Sunday

Monday

Tuesday

Wednesday

Thursday

Friday

Saturday

# January

| | Sunday ☐ |
|---|---|

| | Monday ☐ |
|---|---|

| | Tuesday ☐ |
|---|---|

| | Wednesday ☐ |
|---|---|

| | Thursday ☐ |
|---|---|

| | Friday ☐ |
|---|---|

| | Saturday ☐ |
|---|---|

# January

| | |
|---|---|
| | Sunday ☐ |
| | Monday ☐ |
| | Tuesday ☐ |
| | Wednesday ☐ |
| | Thursday ☐ |
| | Friday ☐ |
| | Saturday ☐ |

# January

| | |
|---|---|
| | Sunday ☐ |
| | Monday ☐ |
| | Tuesday ☐ |
| | Wednesday ☐ |
| | Thursday ☐ |
| | Friday ☐ |
| | Saturday ☐ |

# Notes

# Notes

# FEBRUARY

| Sunday | Monday | Tuesday | Wednesday | Thursday | Friday | Saturday |
|--------|--------|---------|-----------|----------|--------|----------|
|        |        |         |           |          |        |          |
|        |        |         |           |          |        |          |
|        |        |         |           |          |        |          |
|        |        |         |           |          |        |          |
|        |        |         |           |          |        |          |
|        |        |         |           |          |        |          |

# February

Sunday

Monday

Tuesday

Wednesday

Thursday

Friday

Saturday

# February

| | |
|---|---|
| | Sunday ☐ |
| | Monday ☐ |
| | Tuesday ☐ |
| | Wednesday ☐ |
| | Thursday ☐ |
| | Friday ☐ |
| | Saturday ☐ |

# February

- Sunday ☐
- Monday ☐
- Tuesday ☐
- Wednesday ☐
- Thursday ☐
- Friday ☐
- Saturday ☐

# February

Sunday

Monday

Tuesday

Wednesday

Thursday

Friday

Saturday

# February

- Sunday ☐
- Monday ☐
- Tuesday ☐
- Wednesday ☐
- Thursday ☐
- Friday ☐
- Saturday ☐

# Notes

# Notes

# MARCH

| Sunday | Monday | Tuesday | Wednesday | Thursday | Friday | Saturday |
|--------|--------|---------|-----------|----------|--------|----------|
|        |        |         |           |          |        |          |
|        |        |         |           |          |        |          |
|        |        |         |           |          |        |          |
|        |        |         |           |          |        |          |
|        |        |         |           |          |        |          |
|        |        |         |           |          |        |          |

# March

- Sunday ☐
- Monday ☐
- Tuesday ☐
- Wednesday ☐
- Thursday ☐
- Friday ☐
- Saturday ☐

# March

- Sunday ☐
- Monday ☐
- Tuesday ☐
- Wednesday ☐
- Thursday ☐
- Friday ☐
- Saturday ☐

# March

Sunday

Monday

Tuesday

Wednesday

Thursday

Friday

Saturday

# March

| | |
|---|---|
| | Sunday ☐ |
| | Monday ☐ |
| | Tuesday ☐ |
| | Wednesday ☐ |
| | Thursday ☐ |
| | Friday ☐ |
| | Saturday ☐ |

# March

Sunday

Monday

Tuesday

Wednesday

Thursday

Friday

Saturday

# March

| | |
|---|---|
| | Sunday ☐ |
| | Monday ☐ |
| | Tuesday ☐ |
| | Wednesday ☐ |
| | Thursday ☐ |
| | Friday ☐ |
| | Saturday ☐ |

# Notes

# Notes

# APRIL

| Sunday | Monday | Tuesday | Wednesday | Thursday | Friday | Saturday |
|--------|--------|---------|-----------|----------|--------|----------|
|        |        |         |           |          |        |          |
|        |        |         |           |          |        |          |
|        |        |         |           |          |        |          |
|        |        |         |           |          |        |          |
|        |        |         |           |          |        |          |
|        |        |         |           |          |        |          |

## April

- Sunday ☐
- Monday ☐
- Tuesday ☐
- Wednesday ☐
- Thursday ☐
- Friday ☐
- Saturday ☐

# April

Sunday

Monday

Tuesday

Wednesday

Thursday

Friday

Saturday

# April

- Sunday
- Monday
- Tuesday
- Wednesday
- Thursday
- Friday
- Saturday

# April

- Sunday
- Monday
- Tuesday
- Wednesday
- Thursday
- Friday
- Saturday

# April

- Sunday ☐
- Monday ☐
- Tuesday ☐
- Wednesday ☐
- Thursday ☐
- Friday ☐
- Saturday ☐

# Notes

# Notes

# MAY

| Sunday | Monday | Tuesday | Wednesday | Thursday | Friday | Saturday |
|--------|--------|---------|-----------|----------|--------|----------|
|        |        |         |           |          |        |          |
|        |        |         |           |          |        |          |
|        |        |         |           |          |        |          |
|        |        |         |           |          |        |          |
|        |        |         |           |          |        |          |
|        |        |         |           |          |        |          |

# May

- Sunday ☐
- Monday ☐
- Tuesday ☐
- Wednesday ☐
- Thursday ☐
- Friday ☐
- Saturday ☐

# May

Sunday

Monday

Tuesday

Wednesday

Thursday

Friday

Saturday

# May

| | |
|---|---|
| | Sunday ☐ |
| | Monday ☐ |
| | Tuesday ☐ |
| | Wednesday ☐ |
| | Thursday ☐ |
| | Friday ☐ |
| | Saturday ☐ |

# May

| | |
|---|---|
| | Sunday ☐ |
| | Monday ☐ |
| | Tuesday ☐ |
| | Wednesday ☐ |
| | Thursday ☐ |
| | Friday ☐ |
| | Saturday ☐ |

# May

- Sunday ☐
- Monday ☐
- Tuesday ☐
- Wednesday ☐
- Thursday ☐
- Friday ☐
- Saturday ☐

# Notes

# Notes

# JUNE

| Sunday | Monday | Tuesday | Wednesday | Thursday | Friday | Saturday |
|--------|--------|---------|-----------|----------|--------|----------|
|        |        |         |           |          |        |          |
|        |        |         |           |          |        |          |
|        |        |         |           |          |        |          |
|        |        |         |           |          |        |          |
|        |        |         |           |          |        |          |
|        |        |         |           |          |        |          |

# June

Sunday

Monday

Tuesday

Wednesday

Thursday

Friday

Saturday

# June

|  |
|---|
| Sunday ☐ |
| Monday ☐ |
| Tuesday ☐ |
| Wednesday ☐ |
| Thursday ☐ |
| Friday ☐ |
| Saturday ☐ |

# June

| | Sunday ☐ |
|---|---|

| | Monday ☐ |
|---|---|

| | Tuesday ☐ |
|---|---|

| | Wednesday ☐ |
|---|---|

| | Thursday ☐ |
|---|---|

| | Friday ☐ |
|---|---|

| | Saturday ☐ |
|---|---|

# June

- Sunday ☐
- Monday ☐
- Tuesday ☐
- Wednesday ☐
- Thursday ☐
- Friday ☐
- Saturday ☐

# June

- Sunday ☐
- Monday ☐
- Tuesday ☐
- Wednesday ☐
- Thursday ☐
- Friday ☐
- Saturday ☐

# Notes

# Notes

# JULY

| Sunday | Monday | Tuesday | Wednesday | Thursday | Friday | Saturday |
|--------|--------|---------|-----------|----------|--------|----------|
|        |        |         |           |          |        |          |
|        |        |         |           |          |        |          |
|        |        |         |           |          |        |          |
|        |        |         |           |          |        |          |
|        |        |         |           |          |        |          |
|        |        |         |           |          |        |          |

# July

| | |
|---|---|
| | Sunday ☐ |
| | Monday ☐ |
| | Tuesday ☐ |
| | Wednesday ☐ |
| | Thursday ☐ |
| | Friday ☐ |
| | Saturday ☐ |

# July

- [ ] Sunday
- [ ] Monday
- [ ] Tuesday
- [ ] Wednesday
- [ ] Thursday
- [ ] Friday
- [ ] Saturday

# July

Sunday ☐

Monday ☐

Tuesday ☐

Wednesday ☐

Thursday ☐

Friday ☐

Saturday ☐

# July

Sunday

Monday

Tuesday

Wednesday

Thursday

Friday

Saturday

# July

Sunday

Monday

Tuesday

Wednesday

Thursday

Friday

Saturday

# Notes

# Notes

# AUGUST

| Sunday | Monday | Tuesday | Wednesday | Thursday | Friday | Saturday |
|---|---|---|---|---|---|---|
| | | | | | | |
| | | | | | | |
| | | | | | | |
| | | | | | | |
| | | | | | | |
| | | | | | | |

# August

- [ ] Sunday
- [ ] Monday
- [ ] Tuesday
- [ ] Wednesday
- [ ] Thursday
- [ ] Friday
- [ ] Saturday

# August

- Sunday ☐
- Monday ☐
- Tuesday ☐
- Wednesday ☐
- Thursday ☐
- Friday ☐
- Saturday ☐

# August

| | |
|---|---|
| | Sunday ☐ |
| | Monday ☐ |
| | Tuesday ☐ |
| | Wednesday ☐ |
| | Thursday ☐ |
| | Friday ☐ |
| | Saturday ☐ |

# August

- Sunday ☐
- Monday ☐
- Tuesday ☐
- Wednesday ☐
- Thursday ☐
- Friday ☐
- Saturday ☐

# August

Sunday

Monday

Tuesday

Wednesday

Thursday

Friday

Saturday

# August

- Sunday ☐
- Monday ☐
- Tuesday ☐
- Wednesday ☐
- Thursday ☐
- Friday ☐
- Saturday ☐

# Notes

# Notes

# SEPTEMBER

| Sunday | Monday | Tuesday | Wednesday | Thursday | Friday | Saturday |
|--------|--------|---------|-----------|----------|--------|----------|
|        |        |         |           |          |        |          |
|        |        |         |           |          |        |          |
|        |        |         |           |          |        |          |
|        |        |         |           |          |        |          |
|        |        |         |           |          |        |          |
|        |        |         |           |          |        |          |

# September

Sunday

Monday

Tuesday

Wednesday

Thursday

Friday

Saturday

# September

| | |
|---|---|
| | Sunday ☐ |
| | Monday ☐ |
| | Tuesday ☐ |
| | Wednesday ☐ |
| | Thursday ☐ |
| | Friday ☐ |
| | Saturday ☐ |

# September

| | |
|---|---|
| | Sunday ☐ |
| | Monday ☐ |
| | Tuesday ☐ |
| | Wednesday ☐ |
| | Thursday ☐ |
| | Friday ☐ |
| | Saturday ☐ |

# September

- Sunday ☐
- Monday ☐
- Tuesday ☐
- Wednesday ☐
- Thursday ☐
- Friday ☐
- Saturday ☐

# September

- Sunday ☐
- Monday ☐
- Tuesday ☐
- Wednesday ☐
- Thursday ☐
- Friday ☐
- Saturday ☐

# Notes

# Notes

# OCTOBER

| Sunday | Monday | Tuesday | Wednesday | Thursday | Friday | Saturday |
|--------|--------|---------|-----------|----------|--------|----------|
|        |        |         |           |          |        |          |
|        |        |         |           |          |        |          |
|        |        |         |           |          |        |          |
|        |        |         |           |          |        |          |
|        |        |         |           |          |        |          |
|        |        |         |           |          |        |          |

# October

|  |
|---|
| Sunday ☐ |
| Monday ☐ |
| Tuesday ☐ |
| Wednesday ☐ |
| Thursday ☐ |
| Friday ☐ |
| Saturday ☐ |

# October

Sunday

Monday

Tuesday

Wednesday

Thursday

Friday

Saturday

# October

- Sunday ☐
- Monday ☐
- Tuesday ☐
- Wednesday ☐
- Thursday ☐
- Friday ☐
- Saturday ☐

# October

| | |
|---|---|
| | Sunday ☐ |
| | Monday ☐ |
| | Tuesday ☐ |
| | Wednesday ☐ |
| | Thursday ☐ |
| | Friday ☐ |
| | Saturday ☐ |

# October

Sunday

Monday

Tuesday

Wednesday

Thursday

Friday

Saturday

# Notes

# Notes

# NOVEMBER

| Sunday | Monday | Tuesday | Wednesday | Thursday | Friday | Saturday |
|--------|--------|---------|-----------|----------|--------|----------|
|        |        |         |           |          |        |          |
|        |        |         |           |          |        |          |
|        |        |         |           |          |        |          |
|        |        |         |           |          |        |          |
|        |        |         |           |          |        |          |
|        |        |         |           |          |        |          |

# November

| | |
|---|---|
| | Sunday ☐ |
| | Monday ☐ |
| | Tuesday ☐ |
| | Wednesday ☐ |
| | Thursday ☐ |
| | Friday ☐ |
| | Saturday ☐ |

# November

- Sunday ☐
- Monday ☐
- Tuesday ☐
- Wednesday ☐
- Thursday ☐
- Friday ☐
- Saturday ☐

# November

- Sunday ☐
- Monday ☐
- Tuesday ☐
- Wednesday ☐
- Thursday ☐
- Friday ☐
- Saturday ☐

# November

Sunday

Monday

Tuesday

Wednesday

Thursday

Friday

Saturday

# November

- Sunday ☐
- Monday ☐
- Tuesday ☐
- Wednesday ☐
- Thursday ☐
- Friday ☐
- Saturday ☐

# November

| | |
|---|---|
| | Sunday ☐ |
| | Monday ☐ |
| | Tuesday ☐ |
| | Wednesday ☐ |
| | Thursday ☐ |
| | Friday ☐ |
| | Saturday ☐ |

# Notes

# Notes

# DECEMBER

| Sunday | Monday | Tuesday | Wednesday | Thursday | Friday | Saturday |
|--------|--------|---------|-----------|----------|--------|----------|
|        |        |         |           |          |        |          |
|        |        |         |           |          |        |          |
|        |        |         |           |          |        |          |
|        |        |         |           |          |        |          |
|        |        |         |           |          |        |          |
|        |        |         |           |          |        |          |

# November

| | |
|---|---|
| | Sunday ☐ |
| | Monday ☐ |
| | Tuesday ☐ |
| | Wednesday ☐ |
| | Thursday ☐ |
| | Friday ☐ |
| | Saturday ☐ |

# November

| | |
|---|---|
| | Sunday ☐ |
| | Monday ☐ |
| | Tuesday ☐ |
| | Wednesday ☐ |
| | Thursday ☐ |
| | Friday ☐ |
| | Saturday ☐ |

# November

Sunday

Monday

Tuesday

Wednesday

Thursday

Friday

Saturday

# November

Sunday

Monday

Tuesday

Wednesday

Thursday

Friday

Saturday

# November

| | |
|---|---|
| | Sunday ☐ |
| | Monday ☐ |
| | Tuesday ☐ |
| | Wednesday ☐ |
| | Thursday ☐ |
| | Friday ☐ |
| | Saturday ☐ |

# Notes

# Notes

Made in the USA
Monee, IL
04 February 2022